Anne's glory box

Gloria McKinnon

Contents

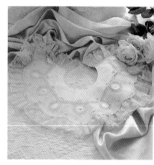

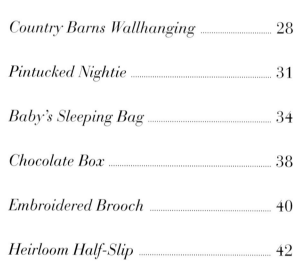

Editorial
Managing Editor: Judy Poulos
Editorial Assistant: Ella Martin
Editorial Coordinator: Margaret Kelly

Photography
Andrew Elton

Styling
Kathy Tripp

Illustrations
Lesley Griffith

Design and Production
Manager: Anna Maguire
Design: Jenny Pace
Layout: Sheridan Packer

Published by J.B. Fairfax Press Pty Limited
80-82 McLachlan Ave
Rushcutters Bay, NSW 2011, Australia
A.C.N. 003 738 430
Formatted by J.B. Fairfax Press Pty Limited
Printed by Toppan Printing Company,
Singapore

JBFP 421

ANNE'S GLORY BOX
Series ISBN 1 86343 166 7
Book 9 ISBN 1 86343 252 3

Anne's Glory Box is our Favourite Destination

Tour groups from all over the world are now making Anne's Glory Box an essential stop on their itinerary. Most recently, I have been delighted to welcome a group of embroiderers from Ube in Japan to the store. This group was visiting Newcastle on a cultural exchange, associated with the sister city programme, and Anne's Glory Box was honoured to be one of the places these ladies requested to visit. The nine members of the group, who are photographed on our back cover, were delighted with the welcome they received.

In August 1996, I will host a Waltzing Matilda tour from the United States. The group will begin their tour at our store, then they will go on to enjoy the delights of the Hunter Valley, followed by a visit to Sydney where they will attend a major needlework show. While the group is in Newcastle, they will do classes with our own tutors while, at the same time, some of the visitors will offer classes to Australian friends of the store. This will be a wonderful exchange of skills and ideas.

Visitors to Anne's Glory Box are always made to feel welcome and we delight in the interest shown by visitors in the store and the high quality of workmanship that we exhibit.

Gloria

All the products shown in this book are available from:
Anne's Glory Box
60-62 Beaumont Street,
Hamilton, Newcastle, NSW 2303
Ph: (049) 61 6016 or Fax: (049) 61 6587

Blossom Basket Quilt

MADE BY YAN PRING

Compose a symphony of springtime with a charming Victorian basket to hold a bouquet of colourwash blooms.

Finished size: 117 cm x 122 cm (46 in x 48 in)

Materials

- ❧ scraps of fabrics including large florals, medium florals, small florals, small leaves and sprigs, large leaves, fabrics for the basket, medium light and very light fabrics for the background, and medium blue fabrics
- ❧ 1.6 m (1³/₄ yd) of lace edging (Yan has used several different laces)
- ❧ 76 cm (30 in) of 1.2 cm (¹/₂ in) wide velvet ribbon for the bow
- ❧ 90 cm (36 in) of cotton bias binding for the handle
- ❧ strips of various widths of fabric for the inner borders
- ❧ 45 cm (18 in) of 140 cm (55 in) wide furnishing cotton for the outer border
- ❧ Perle Cotton to match the velvet ribbon
- ❧ 1.6 m (1³/₄ yd) of low-loft wadding
- ❧ 122 cm x 127 cm (48 in x 50 in) of fabric for the backing
- ❧ 30 cm (12 in) of fabric for the binding

Method

See the Placement Diagram on page 6.

For the colourwash centre

1 Cut a generous selection of fabrics in each category into 5 cm (2 in) squares. Make sure you include yellows, blues and lilacs for a spring bouquet.

2 To make the half-square triangles on the sides of the basket, place a 'basket' square on top of a medium light background square, with the right sides together. Stitch across the diagonal, trim off half of the basket square and flip the other over. Take care to trim the correct half or you will need to begin again (Fig. 1). Press well.

3 Arrange the squares to give a pleasing harmony of colour, following the placement diagram on page 6. Note there are eighteen squares across and twenty squares down. Sew the squares together to form the colourwash centre of the quilt.

For the handle

1 To make the handle, hand-sew the inner edge of the bias binding in place, using a blind hemstitch. Pin the edge of the lace underneath the other side of the handle, then stitch it down, neatening the ends.

2 Tie the velvet ribbon into a bow and attach it to the handle with French knots using the Perle Cotton.

3 Trim the basket with lace as shown.

For the borders

This quilt has been designed so that the basket sits within a lovely frame. Of course, you can design your own borders. To re-create the design shown here, cut your fabrics to the measurements shown on the border diagram on page 6, where each square represents 3.5 cm (1¹/₂ in). Remember to add 1 cm (³/₈ in) for each seam allowance.

Quilting

1 Place the backing face down on a table with the wadding on top and the quilt top on top of that, face upwards. Baste the three layers together securely.

2 Quilt the wallhanging in any pattern you prefer. Yan has quilted only around the borders of her quilt.

Finishing

1 Cut the binding fabric into 5 cm (2 in) wide strips. Join strips together to achieve the required length.

2 Fold the binding over double with the right sides together. Stitch the binding to the top and bottom of the quilt with the raw edges even. Turn the binding to the back of the quilt and slipstitch it in place. Repeat for the sides of the quilt.

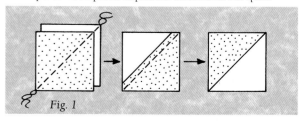

Fig. 1

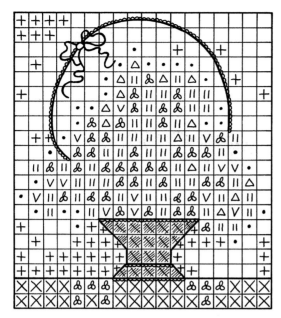

🎀	Large florals	
‖	Medium florals	
△	Small florals	
•	Small leaves and sprigs	
V	Large leaves	
▨	Basket fabrics	
+	Medium light fabrics	
☐	Very light fabrics	
⊠	Medium blue fabrics	

Placement Diagram

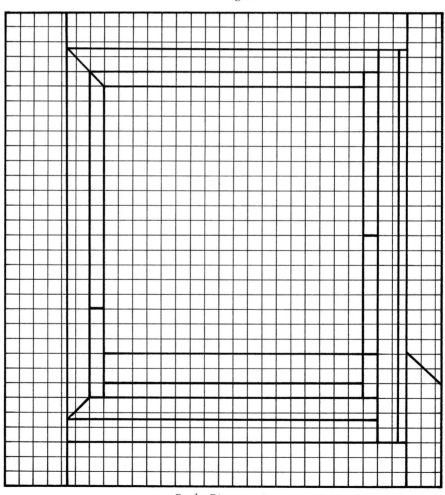

Border Diagram

☐ = 3·5 x 3·5 cm (1½ x 1½ in)

Broida Bear

STITCHED BY SUE MCNEIL

If you love teddy bears, this one is sure to become a favourite, but remember, it is not meant to be a toy.

Materials

- ♣ 20 cm (8 in) of unbleached calico
- ♣ 40 cm (16 in) of 4 cm (1½ in) wide cream cotton lace
- ♣ 50 cm (20 in) of 4 mm (³/₁₆ in) wide silk ribbon
- ♣ two 40 mm (1½ in) buttons
- ♣ four 20 mm (³/₄ in) cream buttons
- ♣ two black beads for the eyes
- ♣ linen thread
- ♣ hat elastic
- ♣ cotton wadding
- ♣ Piecemakers crewel needle, size 10
- ♣ Piecemakers straw needle, size 7 or 9
- ♣ long needle for attaching limbs
- ♣ DMC Stranded Cotton, one skein each: Light Pink 770, Medium Pink 316, Dark Pink 315, Bright Red 3350, Light Blue 932, Medium Blue 931, Light Green 502, Medium Green 501, Dark Green 500, Light Mauve 3743, Medium Mauve 3041, Dark Mauve 3740, Yellow 3078, Black 310
- ♣ tracing paper
- ♣ fineline permanent marking pen
- ♣ pencil

Method

See the Pattern on the Pull Out Pattern Sheet and the Embroidery Design on pages 11-15.

Note: Read all the instructions before you begin. All seams are 6 mm (¼ in) unless stated otherwise.

Sewing

Trace the patterns provided, then cut out the pattern pieces from the calico as directed.

For the ears

1 Place the pieces together with the right sides facing. Stitch around the curved edge, leaving the bottom open. Clip the curves and turn the ears right side out.

2 Turn a small hem at the bottom and slipstitch the edge closed.

For the head

1 Place the side head pieces together with the right sides facing. Stitch from the neck to the nose. Clip the curves.

2 Place the centre gusset and the joined side head together with the right sides facing. Pin the nose points together. Pin the centre back of the gusset to the centre back of one side of the head. Pin that side together around the curve, then stitch. Pin and stitch the other side in the same way. It might be easier to hand-sew around the nose. Clip the curves, then turn the head right side out.

For the body

1 Sew the centre fronts and the centre backs together.

2 Pin the sides together, then stitch, leaving the neck edge open. Turn the body right side out.

For the arms

Pair the arms with the right sides together. Stitch, leaving the opening as indicated on the pattern. Clip the curves and turn the arms right side out.

For the legs

1 Fold the legs with the right sides together. Stitch, leaving an opening as indicated on the pattern and leaving the foot open.

2 Fit the foot pads into the legs, placing one mark at the toe and the other at the heel. Sew the foot pads in place by hand or by machine. Clip the curves and turn the legs right side out.

Stuffing

1 Stuff the arms and legs firmly. Turn a small hem at the opening and close the opening by hand.

2 Stuff the head firmly, making sure there is sufficient stuffing in the nose. With the linen thread, hand-sew a row of gathering stitches 6 mm (1/4 in) from the neck edge. Do not make the gathering stitches too large and leave the thread ends free.

3 Stuff the body firmly, leaving the neck edge closed. Sew a row of gathering around the neck edge as for the head.

Assembling

1 Thread the two 40 mm (1 1/2 in) buttons together with the hat elastic. Tie the elastic off securely so the two buttons can be pulled apart a little.

2 Place one button inside the body. Draw up the gathering on the body so the fabric slides between the two buttons. Tie the thread off securely.

3 Place the other button inside the head and secure it in the same way as for the first button.

Embroidery

Carefully follow the embroidery designs given on pages 11-15.

For the body

1 Work featherstitch in two strands of Light Pink down the centre front and centre back seams from the neck to the crotch. Add the buds in two strands of Medium Pink lazy daisy stitches, surrounded by fly stitches in two strands of Dark Green.

2 Work featherstitch in two strands of Light Green and French knots in two strands of Dark Mauve along the side seams.

3 For the flower embroidery, follow the instructions on the embroidery design.

For the left front

1 Mark the position of the two main roses and the main stems. Work the stems in one strand of Green featherstitch.

2 For the flower embroidery, follow the instructions on the embroidery design.

3 Fill in around the bouquet with more featherstitches. Work fly stitches in one strand of Light Green around the rose buds.

For the right front

1 Mark the positions of the daisies.

2 For the flower embroidery, follow the instructions on the embroidery design.

For the right back

1 Mark the positions of the roses and rose buds.

2 For the flower embroidery, follow the instructions on the embroidery design.

For the left back

1 Mark the positions of the rose buds.

2 For the flower embroidery, follow the instructions on the embroidery design.

For the right arm

1 Work closed buttonhole stitch in two strands of Light Green around the seam of the arm. Work French knots in two strands of Dark Mauve at the points. Work a fan with three straight stitches in two strands of Medium Pink at the top of each French knot.

2 For the flower embroidery, follow the instructions on the embroidery design.

For the left arm

1 Work long and short buttonhole stitches in two strands of Medium Pink around the seam. Work two lazy daisy stitches in two strands of Medium Green at the tops of the long stitches. Work a French knot in one strand of Light Pink between the lazy daisy stitches.

2 For the flower embroidery, follow the instructions on the embroidery design.

For the right leg

1 Work a variation of long and short buttonhole stitches in two strands of Dark Pink around the seam. Work fly stitches in two strands of Light Green at the tops of the long buttonhole stitches. Work a French knot in one strand of Light Pink between the fly stitches.

2 For the flower embroidery, follow the instructions on the embroidery design.

For the right foot

1 Work buttonhole stitches in two strands of Light Pink around the foot pad. Work French knots in two strands of Dark Green around the foot pad.

2 For the flower embroidery, follow the instructions on the embroidery design.

For the left leg

1 Work slanted buttonhole stitch in two strands of Medium Mauve around the seam. Work a cross stitch in two strands of Medium Green at the top of every second buttonhole stitch. Work a French knot in one strand of Dark Pink at the top of the cross.

2 Mark the positions of all the main flowers. For the embroidery, follow the instructions on the embroidery design.

For the left foot

Work open buttonhole stitch in two strands of Dark Mauve around the foot pad. Work French knots in two strands of Light Green around the foot pad.

For the right paw

1 Mark the line for the paw from seam to seam, then embroider in two strands of Medium Pink chain stitch.

2 For the flower embroidery, follow the instructions on the embroidery design.

For the left paw

1 Mark the line for the paw from seam to seam, then embroider in two strands of Dark Mauve chain stitch.

2 For the flower embroidery, follow the instructions on the embroidery design.

For the ears

1 Work open buttonhole stitch in two strands of Medium Pink around the outer edge.

2 For the flower embroidery, follow the instructions on the embroidery design for the left and right ears.

For the nose

1 Using the pencil, mark the nose, following figure 1. Work straight stitches in three strands of Black, making a V-shape from the nose seam downwards. Fill in with straight stitches across the top.

2 Take the thread from the lowest point of the nose down to the position of the mouth. Take a stitch to one side, then to the other side to form the mouth. Finish the thread by bringing it out through the worked nose area.

For the eyes

1 Using the linen thread, introduce the needle at the centre back base of the head, then take it through to the position of the eye. Thread a bead on, then take the needle back to the entry point, pulling the thread firmly.

2 Insert the needle again, a stitch away and attach the other eye. Make sure the two eyes are set evenly, then tie off the threads.

Attaching the limbs

1 Knot the end of a doubled length of linen thread. Using the long needle, stitch from the arm placement mark on one side of the body to the arm placement mark on the other side.

2 Push the needle through the arm, then thread one of the cream buttons on the outside. Take the thread back through the button to the starting point.

3 Stitch through the button to the other side, then attach the other arm and button. Take the thread back through the button, arm and body to the other side, bringing it out between the body and the arm. Pull in the arm against the body to match the other arm.

4 Loop the thread around between the arm and the body and pass the needle through the loop. Do this several times to make sure it is quite secure, then cut the thread.

5 Attach the legs in the same way as the arms.

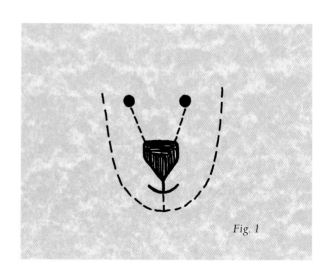

Fig. 1

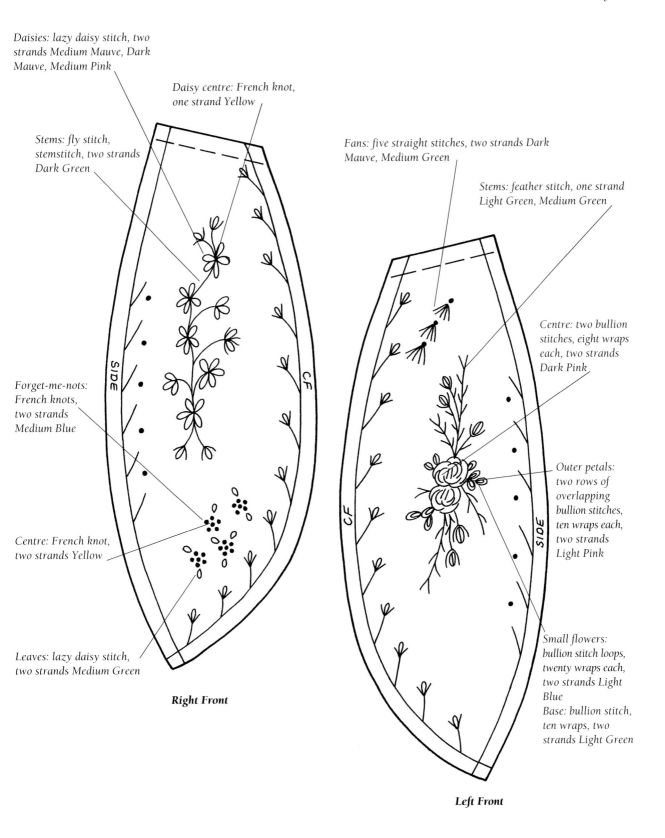

Daisies: lazy daisy stitch, two strands Medium Mauve, Dark Mauve, Medium Pink

Daisy centre: French knot, one strand Yellow

Stems: fly stitch, stemstitch, two strands Dark Green

Fans: five straight stitches, two strands Dark Mauve, Medium Green

Stems: feather stitch, one strand Light Green, Medium Green

Centre: two bullion stitches, eight wraps each, two strands Dark Pink

Forget-me-nots: French knots, two strands Medium Blue

Outer petals: two rows of overlapping bullion stitches, ten wraps each, two strands Light Pink

Centre: French knot, two strands Yellow

Leaves: lazy daisy stitch, two strands Medium Green

Small flowers: bullion stitch loops, twenty wraps each, two strands Light Blue
Base: bullion stitch, ten wraps, two strands Light Green

Right Front

Left Front

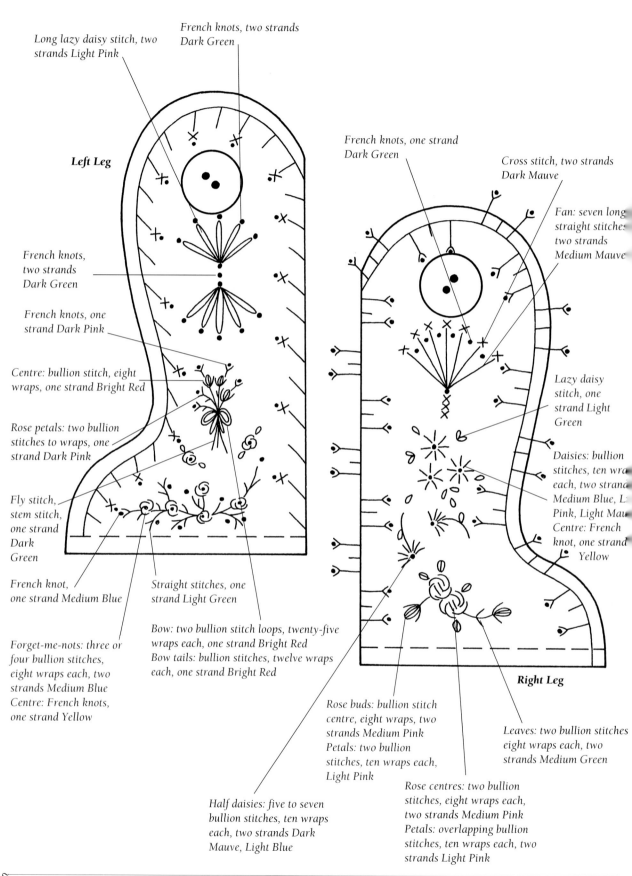

Long lazy daisy stitch, two strands Light Pink

French knots, two strands Dark Green

Left Leg

French knots, one strand Dark Green

Cross stitch, two strands Dark Mauve

Fan: seven long straight stitches, two strands Medium Mauve

French knots, two strands Dark Green

French knots, one strand Dark Pink

Centre: bullion stitch, eight wraps, one strand Bright Red

Rose petals: two bullion stitches to wraps, one strand Dark Pink

Fly stitch, stem stitch, one strand Dark Green

French knot, one strand Medium Blue

Straight stitches, one strand Light Green

Forget-me-nots: three or four bullion stitches, eight wraps each, two strands Medium Blue Centre: French knots, one strand Yellow

Bow: two bullion stitch loops, twenty-five wraps each, one strand Bright Red
Bow tails: bullion stitches, twelve wraps each, one strand Bright Red

Lazy daisy stitch, one strand Light Green

Daisies: bullion stitches, ten wraps each, two strands Medium Blue, Light Pink, Light Mauve
Centre: French knot, one strand Yellow

Leaves: two bullion stitches eight wraps each, two strands Medium Green

Right Leg

Rose buds: bullion stitch centre, eight wraps, two strands Medium Pink
Petals: two bullion stitches, ten wraps each, Light Pink

Half daisies: five to seven bullion stitches, ten wraps each, two strands Dark Mauve, Light Blue

Rose centres: two bullion stitches, eight wraps each, two strands Medium Pink
Petals: overlapping bullion stitches, ten wraps each, two strands Light Pink

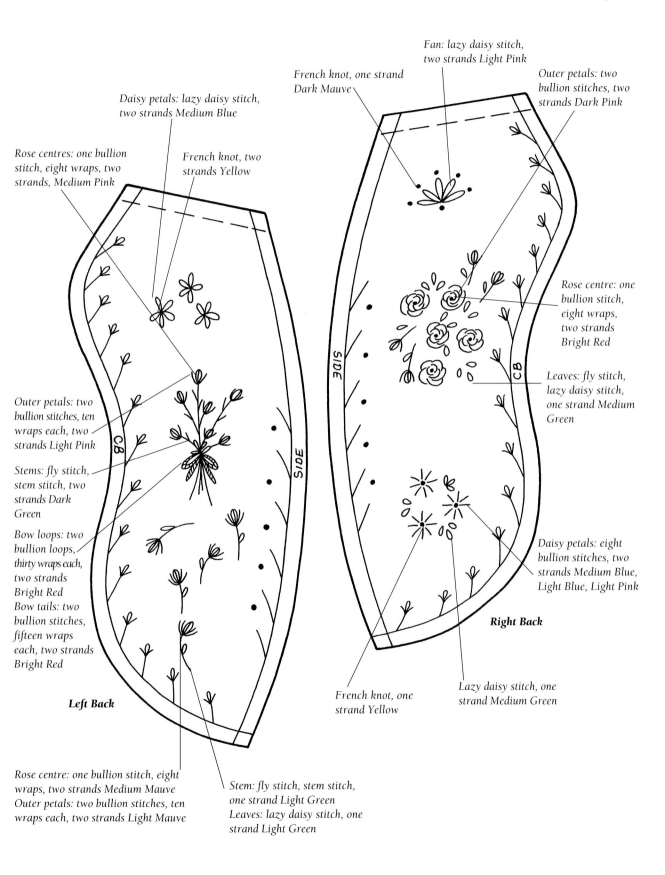

Fan: lazy daisy stitch,
two strands Light Pink

French knot, one strand
Dark Mauve

Outer petals: two
bullion stitches, two
strands Dark Pink

Daisy petals: lazy daisy stitch,
two strands Medium Blue

Rose centres: one bullion
stitch, eight wraps, two
strands, Medium Pink

French knot, two
strands Yellow

Rose centre: one
bullion stitch,
eight wraps,
two strands
Bright Red

Leaves: fly stitch,
lazy daisy stitch,
one strand Medium
Green

Outer petals: two
bullion stitches, ten
wraps each, two
strands Light Pink

Stems: fly stitch,
stem stitch, two
strands Dark
Green

Bow loops: two
bullion loops,
thirty wraps each,
two strands
Bright Red
Bow tails: two
bullion stitches,
fifteen wraps
each, two strands
Bright Red

Daisy petals: eight
bullion stitches, two
strands Medium Blue,
Light Blue, Light Pink

Right Back

French knot, one
strand Yellow

Lazy daisy stitch, one
strand Medium Green

Left Back

Rose centre: one bullion stitch, eight
wraps, two strands Medium Mauve
Outer petals: two bullion stitches, ten
wraps each, two strands Light Mauve

Stem: fly stitch, stem stitch,
one strand Light Green
Leaves: lazy daisy stitch, one
strand Light Green

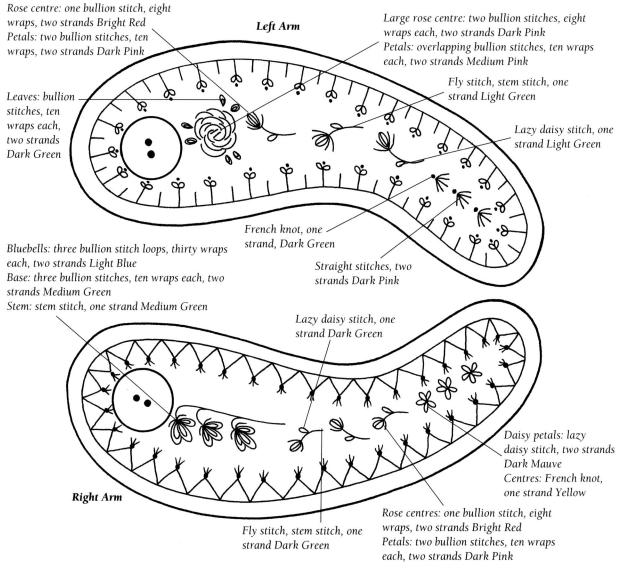

Left Arm

Rose centre: one bullion stitch, eight wraps, two strands Bright Red
Petals: two bullion stitches, ten wraps, two strands Dark Pink

Large rose centre: two bullion stitches, eight wraps each, two strands Dark Pink
Petals: overlapping bullion stitches, ten wraps each, two strands Medium Pink

Leaves: bullion stitches, ten wraps each, two strands Dark Green

Fly stitch, stem stitch, one strand Light Green

Lazy daisy stitch, one strand Light Green

Bluebells: three bullion stitch loops, thirty wraps each, two strands Light Blue
Base: three bullion stitches, ten wraps each, two strands Medium Green
Stem: stem stitch, one strand Medium Green

French knot, one strand, Dark Green

Straight stitches, two strands Dark Pink

Lazy daisy stitch, one strand Dark Green

Daisy petals: lazy daisy stitch, two strands Dark Mauve
Centres: French knot, one strand Yellow

Right Arm

Fly stitch, stem stitch, one strand Dark Green

Rose centres: one bullion stitch, eight wraps, two strands Bright Red
Petals: two bullion stitches, ten wraps each, two strands Dark Pink

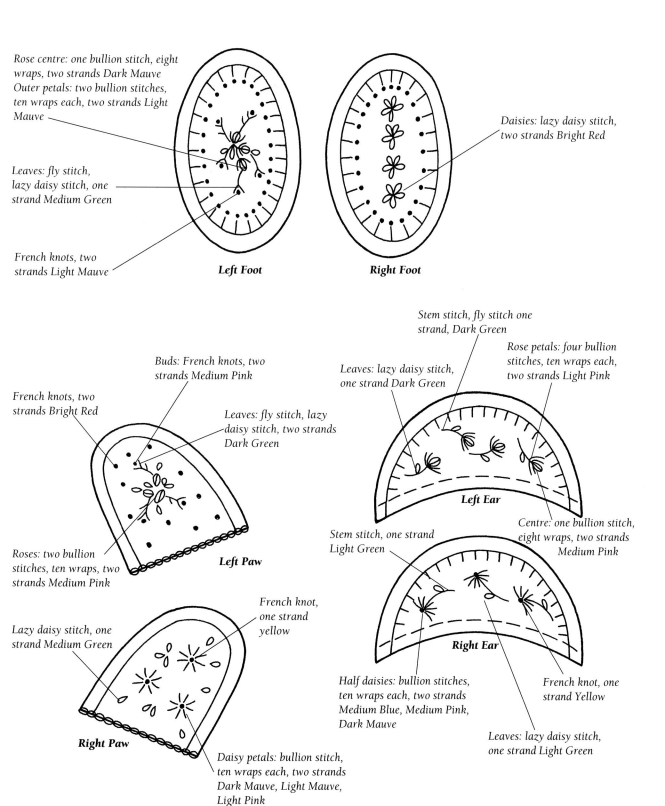

Rose centre: one bullion stitch, eight wraps, two strands Dark Mauve
Outer petals: two bullion stitches, ten wraps each, two strands Light Mauve

Leaves: fly stitch, lazy daisy stitch, one strand Medium Green

French knots, two strands Light Mauve

Left Foot

Daisies: lazy daisy stitch, two strands Bright Red

Right Foot

Buds: French knots, two strands Medium Pink

French knots, two strands Bright Red

Leaves: fly stitch, lazy daisy stitch, two strands Dark Green

Roses: two bullion stitches, ten wraps, two strands Medium Pink

Left Paw

Lazy daisy stitch, one strand Medium Green

French knot, one strand yellow

Right Paw

Daisy petals: bullion stitch, ten wraps each, two strands Dark Mauve, Light Mauve, Light Pink

Stem stitch, fly stitch one strand, Dark Green

Leaves: lazy daisy stitch, one strand Dark Green

Rose petals: four bullion stitches, ten wraps each, two strands Light Pink

Left Ear

Centre: one bullion stitch, eight wraps, two strands Medium Pink

Stem stitch, one strand Light Green

French knot, one strand Yellow

Right Ear

Half daisies: bullion stitches, ten wraps each, two strands Medium Blue, Medium Pink, Dark Mauve

Leaves: lazy daisy stitch, one strand Light Green

Fuchsia Pillow

STITCHED BY MERRILYN HEAZLEWOOD

This pillow is another of Merrilyn's delightful designs featuring silk ribbon embroidered flowers.

Materials

- ❧ 33 cm (13 in) square of blue/grey Jobelan fabric
- ❧ 3 m (3¼ yd) of 7 cm (2¾ in) wide white cotton lace
- ❧ 75 cm (30 in) of plum cotton fabric
- ❧ chenille needle, size 18
- ❧ 1 m (1⅛ yd) each of 7 mm (⁵/₁₆ in) wide silk ribbon: Palest Pink, Mauve, Pink, Deep Pink, Deep Purple, Coral
- ❧ 2 m (2¼ yd) each of 7 mm (⁵/₁₆ in) wide silk ribbon: White, Green
- ❧ DMC Stranded Cotton: 327, 3712, White
- ❧ DMC Perle Cotton: 8, 369
- ❧ polyester fibre fill

Method

1 Using the chenille needle and following figures 1 to 3, work the fuchsias on the pillow front in the colours indicated. Note that the base of the flower is made up of five straight stitches worked in a fan shape, with the centre stitch worked last. The three top petals are worked in ribbon stitch (Fig. 4). Again, work the centre stitch last. When working ribbon stitch, take care not to pull the ribbon through too firmly, but allow it to sit softly so that the end curls over.

2 For the pistil, work a straight stitch with a French knot at the end in two strands of cotton.

3 For the stamens, work four straight stitches, using one strand of cotton.

4 For the buds, work two straight stitches sitting virtually on top of each other, then couch the ribbons with one strand of White cotton approximately a quarter of the way down from the top. Stitch over the ribbons several times.

5 For the leaves, work ribbon stitches.

6 For the flower stems, work straight stitches with the Perle Cotton.

Finishing

1 Cut three 14 cm (5½ in) wide strips across the full width of the plum fabric for the frill. From the remaining fabric, cut a 33 cm (13 in) square for the back of the pillow.

2 Join the frill lengths into a loop. Fold the loop over double with the wrong sides together. Pin the lace to the frill, matching the raw edges. Gather the frill and the lace together with two rows of gathering. Pin the frill around the pillow front with the raw edges even. Adjust the gathering, placing a little extra fullness at the corners. Stitch the frill in place.

3 Place the pillow front and back together with the right sides facing. Stitch around in the stitching line of the frill, leaving a small opening. Turn the pillow through to the right side. Stuff quite firmly, then close the opening by hand.

Merrilyn Heazlewood has introduced thousands of needlewomen to the delights of silk ribbon embroidery through her books: *Spring Bulb Sampler, Fuchsia, Roses, Cottage Garden, Floral Embellishments* and *Romantic Garden.*

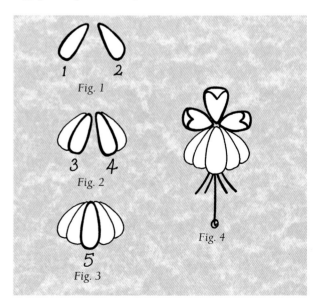

1 2
Fig. 1

3 4
Fig. 2

5
Fig. 3

Fig. 4

Easter Posy Blanket

MADE BY ANNE'S GLORY BOX

A posy of pink roses and Easter daisies makes a pretty piece to lay over the back of your favourite chair.

Materials

- ❧ 80 cm (32 in) of blanket wool
- ❧ 1 m (1⅛ yd) of 140 cm (55 in) wide or 1.4 m (1½ yd) of 115 cm (45 in) wide backing fabric
- ❧ 4.2 m (4½ yd) of 2.5 cm (1 in) wide silk ribbon, Pink
- ❧ 9.5 m (10½ yd) of 2.5 cm (1 in) wide silk ribbon, Pale Pink
- ❧ 1 m (1⅛ yd) of 2.5 cm (1 in) wide silk ribbon, Blue
- ❧ 5 m (5½ yd) of 4 mm (³/₁₆ in) wide silk ribbon, Yellow
- ❧ Piecemakers tapestry needle, size 22
- ❧ Appleton's Crewel Wool: two skeins each of Brilliant White and Pale Blue, one skein of Pale Lemon
- ❧ Gossamer Mohair Wool, two skeins of Green
- ❧ water-soluble marker pen

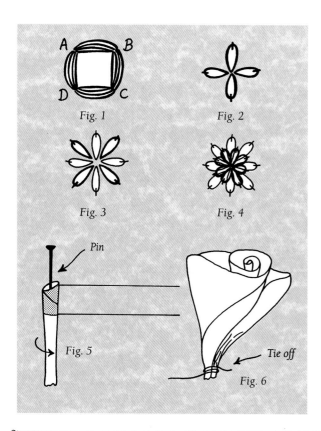

Fig. 1

Fig. 2

Fig. 3

Fig. 4

Pin

Fig. 5

Tie off

Fig. 6

Method

See the Embroidery Design on the Pull Out Pattern Sheet.

Embroidery

1 Using the marker pen, lightly draw the stems and leaves on the centre of the blanket wool.

2 Embroider the leaves and leaf stems in stem stitch. For the main stems work three rows of stem stitch very close together. Stitch the main vein on each leaf in stem stitch and the smaller veins in a single straight stitch.

For the forget-me-nots

1 Using one strand of Pale Blue Appleton's Wool, work a small straight stitch from A to B over approximately two threads of the blanket wool. Work another three straight stitches from A to B, each time laying the stitch away from the centre of the flower. Stitch B to C, C to D, and D to A in the same way (Fig. 1).

2 For the centre, work a French knot using one strand of Pale Lemon.

For the Easter daisies

1 Fill all the remaining space in the entire centre of the posy with Easter daisies. These daisies are stitched using one strand of Brilliant White and working two rounds of lazy daisy stitch, following figures 2, 3 and 4. Note that the second round of lazy daisy stitch has eight shorter petals placed between the first round.

2 For the centres of the daisies, work a French knot in Yellow silk ribbon.

For the roses

1 The roses should be placed last of all. You will need at least fifteen roses, five of which should be larger than the others. Use the darker pink ribbon for the centre of the rose and the lighter pink for the outer petals. Fold over the end of the darker pink ribbon (Fig. 5).

2 Begin rolling the ribbon around this centre. Using the matching thread, stitch through the base of the rose to secure it (Fig. 6).

3 Continue to fold and roll the ribbon until the centre is the size you want. Turn the ribbon down and stitch it to the base.

4 Fold over the end of the paler ribbon and continue to fold and roll it around the centre. Do not keep these petals too tight but allow them to stand out a little.

5 When the rose is the desired size, cut the ribbon and stitch the end to the base, but do not cut the thread. Leave a long tail so you can use the same thread to attach the rose to the blanket wool.

Finishing

1 Lay the backing fabric face down on a hard surface. Centre the embroidered blanket wool, face upwards, on top. There should be a 10 cm (4 in) border of the backing fabric showing all around.

2 Baste the blanket wool to the backing horizontally, vertically and diagonally.

3 Fold the backing fabric to meet the edge of the blanket wool, then fold it again so the folded edge is over the edge of the blanket wool. Pin the folded edge in place, mitring the corners. Slipstitch the backing to the blanket wool, but take care not to stitch through to the back. Stitch the mitres.

Hussif

MADE BY MONICA M. HUNT

Traditionally, a folding bag or roll taken by men going to war in 1914-18, the hussif is a useful way to keep all your sewing tools at hand.

With a name that may be a corruption of 'housewife', the hussif was seen to replace the sewing and mending services usually performed by a housewife, with a pincushion and compartments for thimble, tape measure, buttons and scissors. The original hussif was made in the form of a sleeve which kept all the equipment handy while leaving both hands free to work. Many of the original hussifs were very decorative.

Materials

- ♣ 50 cm (20 in) of Liberty print fabric for the outer cover
- ♣ 50 cm (20 in) of plain lightweight fabric for the lining (it is best to use a natural fibre, not a synthetic one)
- ♣ 18 cm x 44 cm (7 in x 17$\frac{1}{2}$ in) of Pellon
- ♣ small amount of polyester fibre fill
- ♣ 50 cm (20 in) of lightweight iron-on Vilene
- ♣ small amount of flannel for the needlebook
- ♣ straw needle, largest size
- ♣ Piecemakers crewel embroidery needles, size 8 or 9
- ♣ invisible press stud
- ♣ wooden beads or little buttons
- ♣ small piece of soft leather or chamois
- ♣ matching sewing thread
- ♣ fineline permanent marker pen
- ♣ an assortment of coloured embroidery threads to complement the outer fabric including Perle No. 5 and a stranded cotton for button loops etc in the same colour

Method

See the Patterns on the Pull Out Pattern Sheet.

Note: Compartments can be made from either the lining fabric or the Liberty.

1 Cut out the following pieces: the long hussif, 22 cm x 64 cm (8$\frac{5}{8}$ in x 25$\frac{3}{8}$ in) from the Liberty fabric; the piece for quilting, 18 cm x 60 cm (7 in x 23$\frac{5}{8}$ in), from the lining fabric; the sleeve, 18 cm x 42 cm (7 in x 16$\frac{1}{2}$ in) from the lining fabric and 18 cm x 20 cm (7 in x 7$\frac{7}{8}$ in) from the Vilene; the button pocket, 10 cm x 37 cm (4 in x 14$\frac{1}{2}$ in) from the lining or the outer fabric.

2 Cut out the pattern pieces as indicated on the pattern sheet.

3 On the piece for quilting, place the Pellon on the back of the fabric piece. Baste them together, then quilt 44 cm (17$\frac{1}{2}$ in) of the length of the piece in a square grid.

4 On the sleeve, press the Vilene onto the middle of the fabric piece. Join the two short ends of the piece with a 1 cm (³/₈ in) seam.

For the needlebook

For the outer fabric and lining section, press the Vilene onto the back of both pieces then place them together with the right sides facing and sew around the edge with a 5 mm (³/₁₆ in) seam, leaving a small opening for turning. Turn the piece to the right side and press carefully.

For the thimble pocket

Press the Vilene piece onto one end of the fabric piece. Fold the piece along the fold line with the right sides together. Sew around the edge with a 5 mm ($^3/_{16}$ in) seam, leaving a small opening for turning. Turn the piece to the right side and press carefully.

For the scissors holder

Make the scissors holder in the same way as the thimble pocket.

For the button pocket

Fold the button pocket in half along the long side. Cut out a piece of Vilene, using the pattern provided. Press the Vilene onto one half, placing the round end at the fold. Sew around the edge in the shape of the Vilene, leaving a small opening for turning. Trim the corners, turn and press.

For the tape pocket

Iron the tape pocket A piece of Vilene onto the middle of the fabric piece (Fig.1). Fold in the fabric around the edge to the shape of the Vilene. Press well. Press tape pocket B piece of Vilene over the tape pocket A with the folds sandwiched in between. Press it in place. Mitre the two corners at one end, stitching the mitres into place with small slipstitches.

For the pincushion

1 Iron the Vilene onto the backs of the fabric pieces. Sew them together with a 5 mm ($^3/_{16}$ in) seam, with the right sides facing and leaving a small opening. Turn and press. Stuff the pincushion with the fibre fill, then close the opening.

Note: Now you must decide which side will be the top of your pincushion. Take into account where you will place your embroidery and how much you are planning to do.

2 Thread the straw needle with a 160 cm (63 in) length of the Perle No. 5 thread and knot one end. Measure across the diameter of the pincushion at two angles and mark the point where these lines intersect (the centre) with a pin. Do the same on the other side. Pass the needle through the centre of the top of the pincushion, pulling hard to take the knot into the stuffing. Take the needle through to the centre of the bottom. Pulling the thread very, very firmly, divide the pincushion into half, then quarters, then eighths by wrapping the thread around and passing it back through the centre. It is important that you pull the thread hard in order to create the pumpkin-like shape. When you have made the last wrap, finishing at the bottom of the pincushion, make a small buttonhole stitch bar across the threads, then finish off by passing the thread back through the pincushion.

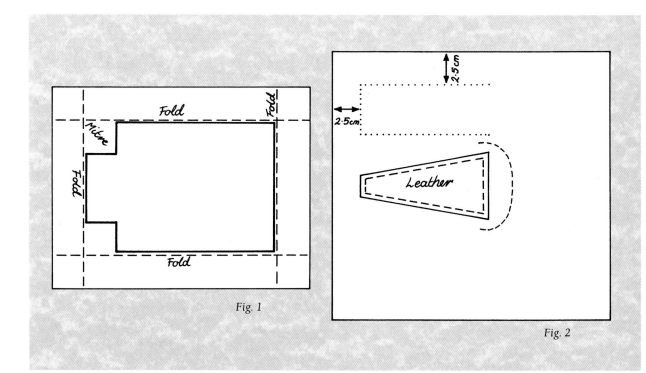

Fig. 1

Fig. 2

Embroidery

1 Using double knot stitch, the straw needle and the Perle No. 5 thread, embroider around the needlebook, the scissors holder and the thimble pocket. Fold the button pocket and the thimble pocket into small bag shapes, then work along the sides in double knot stitch to join them. Work around the pincushion in double knot stitch, taking care to slip the needle under the binding to keep the pumpkin shape.

2 Using two strands of cotton, work double feather stitch across the two short ends of the sleeve.

3 A third of the way down the back of the thimble pocket, work a small buttonhole stitch bar. Work two small buttonhole stitch bars on the back of the button pocket. Work around the three Vilene-backed flannel pieces with buttonhole stitch.

4 Embellish the compartments with your choice of embroidery. Taking your inspiration from the outer fabric always gives a pretty effect.

Finishing

1 Press the sleeve piece flat with the seam at the centre back. Measure down 2.5 cm (1 in) from the top and left side. Using the marker pen, mark these lines with small dots (Fig. 2). Using a basting stitch, sew the tape pocket in place, between the dotted lines.

2 Trim the leather or chamois to the shape of the scissors holder. Hand-sew one half to the back of the scissors holder, then fold the leather in half. Position the scissors holder on the sleeve, then sew the free half of the leather or chamois to the sleeve. Sew the scissors holder to the sleeve.

3 Attach the button pocket, thimble pocket and pincushion to the sleeve by sewing through the bar on the back.

4 Make a 10 cm (4 in) cord from the remaining Perle No. 5 thread. Fold over one end to make a small slug and stitch to secure. Sew this to the top of the invisible press stud. Sew the other end of the cord through the sleeve. This little cord is for holding the scissors in place.

5 Place the long hussif and the quilted piece together with the wrong sides facing. Roll in the sides of the long hussif to cover the edges of the quilted piece and baste them in place. Measure down 15 cm ($5^7/8$ in) and open the stitching to fit the sleeve into place, then rebaste.

6 Starting at the top right-hand corner, using the crewel needle and two strands of cotton, work double feather stitch all around, securing the rolled edge and the sleeve as you go. Remove the basting.

7 At the bottom edge, fold up 11.5 cm ($4^1/2$ in) forming a pocket. Sew the sides with double knot stitch.

8 Sew the flannel pieces to the needlebook, then attach the needlebook over the quilted piece.

9 Cover two wooden beads with the remaining Perle No. 5. Make buttonhole stitch bars at the top of the hussif. Roll up to position the beads, then sew on the beads.

Stitch Guide

Double knot stitch

Pull the thread through from the back at **A**. Insert the needle at **B**, bringing it up again at **C**. Pull the thread through (Fig. 1).

Without piercing the fabric, run the needle under the stitch and pull the thread through (Fig. 2).

Make a loop as shown and again run the needle under the stitch at **B** and over the thread at **C**. Pull the thread through (Fig. 3).

For a single stitch, take the needle to the back of the work at **D** (Fig. 4). For a sequence, carry the thread to the position of the next stitch and repeat (Fig. 5).

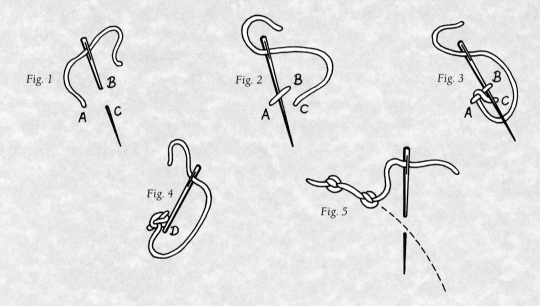

Double feather stitch

Pull the thread through from the fabric at **A**, inserting it at **B** and making a loop as shown. Bring the needle out at **C**, keeping the thread beneath the needle. Pull the thread through (Fig. 1).

Insert the needle at **D** bringing it out again at **E**, making a loop as shown. Again, keep the thread under the needle (Fig. 2).

Insert the needle at **F**, bringing it out at **G** and making a loop as before (Fig. 3).

Insert the needle at **H**, bringing it out at **I** and making a loop as before (Fig. 4). Continue working in this way, placing two stitches to the right and two stitches to the left. Secure the last stitch with a small stitch over the loop.

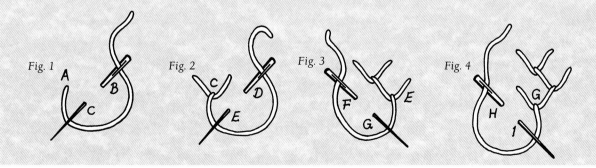

Rose Blush Collar

MADE BY WENDY LEE RAGAN

Trimmed with lace and delicate embroidery, this pretty collar makes a delightful accessory for a little girl's dress.

Materials

- ♣ 25 cm x 115 cm (10 in x 45 in) of white Swiss batiste
- ♣ 30 cm x 115 cm (12 in x 45 in) of pink Swiss batiste
- ♣ 2.7 m (3 yd) of 1-1.5 cm ($^3/_8$-$^5/_8$ in) wide insertion lace
- ♣ 3 m (3$^1/_4$ yd) of 1.5 cm ($^5/_8$ in) wide or wider lace edging
- ♣ 1.37 m (1$^1/_2$ yd) of entredeux
- ♣ Anchor Embroidery Floss: White, China Rose Very Light, Cobalt Blue Light, Juniper Very Light, Citrus Very Light
- ♣ small pearl button
- ♣ matching sewing thread
- ♣ tracing paper
- ♣ fineline permanent marker pen
- ♣ water-soluble marker pen
- ♣ cork board or something similar
- ♣ spray starch

Method

See the Pattern and the Lace-Shaping Pattern on the Pull Out Pattern Sheet.

1 Cut the white Swiss batiste in half to form two rectangles, each approximately 25 cm x 57.5 cm (10 in x 22$^1/_2$ in).

2 Spray the fabric with starch and press. Onto one rectangle, trace the pattern of the collar from the neckline to the bottom of the loops of insertion lace, using the water-soluble pen.

3 Place the two pieces of white fabric with the right sides together. Stitch along the seam line of the neck. Trim carefully around the collar, leaving a 6 mm ($^1/_4$ in) seam allowance all around. From here on, treat the two layers as a single piece.

4 Trace the lace shaping pattern from the pattern sheet, using the permanent marker pen and pin the pattern to the cork board or something similar. Pin the collar piece over the pattern and shape the insertion lace, following the pattern. Baste the lace to the fabric, then press with a moderate iron so as not to damage the delicate lace.

5 Attach the lace by machine-stitching with a tiny straight stitch in the header of the lace. You can now stitch around the lace with a tiny zigzag stitch or a pinstitch. Do not stitch the bottom edge of the loops of lace. Carefully cut away the remaining Swiss batiste from beneath the lace. Spray the collar with starch and press carefully, retaining the shape of the loops of lace.

6 Cut the pink Swiss batiste into two rectangles. Spray with starch and press, as for the white fabric. Pin one piece of the pink fabric over the pattern on the board and trace the bottom of the pattern onto the fabric, using the water-soluble pen. Draw the bottom edge of the lace insertion loops for placement.

7 Place the two pieces of pink batiste together. From here on, treat them as a single piece. Place the white collar on top of the pink piece and pin it into place.

8 Baste the insertion lace to the pink batiste. Machine-stitch the lace into place with a tiny straight stitch in the header of the lace. Zigzag or pinstitch the bottom lace loops to the pink batiste. Cut away the remaining pink batiste above the insertion lace loops.

9 Staystitch the outside edges of the collar, following the curves and points. Attach the entredeux to the outside edge of the collar. You can also attach entredeux to the centre back edges of the collar, if you wish.

10 Embroider the roses, rose buds and feather stitching, following the design on the pattern and stitching through both layers of fabric.

11 Gather the lace edging. Attach the edging to the entredeux, stitching by hand or by machine.

12 Make a small buttonhole loop at the neck edge. Sew on the button to correspond.

Country Barns Wallhanging

MADE BY FAY KING

This small hand-pieced quilted wallhanging is a great way to use a lot of country-style fabrics from your scrap bag.

Finished size: 96 cm x 105 cm (38 in x 41 in)

Materials

- ❦ small pieces of floral, checked and striped fabric for the barns (you can make each barn the same or each one quite different)
- ❦ Piecemakers crewel needles, size 9
- ❦ cotton threads to match the fabrics
- ❦ 1 m (1^1/$_8$ yd) of fabric for the backing
- ❦ 100 cm x 109 cm (39 in x 43 in) of wadding
- ❦ 25 cm (10 in) of navy fabric for the first border
- ❦ 35 cm (14 in) of fabric for the second border
- ❦ cardboard for the templates
- ❦ H or HB propelling pencil
- ❦ ruler

Method

See the Templates on the Pull Out Pattern Sheet.

Preparation

Trace the templates from the pattern sheet. Transfer each one to the cardboard and carefully cut it out. Make nine cardboard templates for each shape.

For each barn

1 Place each cardboard template onto the back of a fabric piece and draw around it. Cut out the piece, adding a 6 mm (^{1}/$_4$ in) seam allowance. Take special care when cutting out the barn roof as it will only fit if cut one way.

2 Baste the fabric over the cardboard, making sure that it sits square and straight.

Hint: When basting the fabric over the cardboard, centre the cardboard on the wrong side of the fabric, then fold and stitch

until it is quite secure, placing a stitch to hold any fabric folds. For triangles, do not try to fold in all the fabric at the corners. Simply fold over the seam allowance and baste it in place, leaving a flap of fabric at the corner. This will give you nice sharp points with not too much bulk.

3 When all the cardboard pieces for one block have been covered, lay the block out, ready for assembly. Place the first two pieces to be joined with the right sides together. Begin stitching approximately 6 mm (^{1}/$_4$ in) from the left-hand corner, stitch up to that corner, then down to the right-hand corner. Topstitch back along the seam for approximately 6 mm (^{1}/$_4$ in) to secure. Snip the thread, leaving a tail approximately 6 mm (^{1}/$_4$ in) long. When you are stitching, catch only the fabric, not the cardboard. Join all the other pieces for the block in this way. Make nine blocks.

Assembling

1 Cut six pieces of cardboard for the sashing, each 5 cm x 25 cm (2 in x 10 in). Cut the fabric and cover the cardboard in the same way as for the barns.

2 Join three blocks together in a row with a length of sashing in between.

3 Join three rows together to form the centre of the quilt, taking care that all the corners meet accurately.

For the first border

1 Measure the width and length of the quilt. Cut cardboard strips 4 cm (1^1/$_2$ in) wide and these lengths. Cut the navy fabric and cover the cardboard strips as before.

2 Cut 4 cm (1^1/$_2$ in) squares from the cardboard for the corners. Cut out the fabric and cover the cardboard squares as before.

3 Attach one square to each end of the top and bottom borders, then attach the side borders.

For the outer border

1 Measure the quilt carefully, then cut cardboard and fabric to these measurements as before.

2 Attach the side borders to the quilt, then the top and bottom borders.

Finishing

1 Carefully remove all the cardboard pieces by undoing or snipping all the basting threads. Press the quilt top well.

2 Baste under the seam allowances around the edges of the quilt.

3 Lay the backing face down on a table with the wadding on top and the quilt top on top of that, face upwards. Baste the layers together securely.

4 Quilt around the pieces as indicated in the quilting diagram below or in a design of your own.

5 Trim the backing to 2.5 cm (1 in) bigger than the quilt top all around. Trim the wadding to the exact size of the quilt top. Fold the excess backing over the wadding, under the edge of the quilt top. Slipstitch the edges together.

6 Make a sleeve for the back of the wallhanging so you can hang it up.

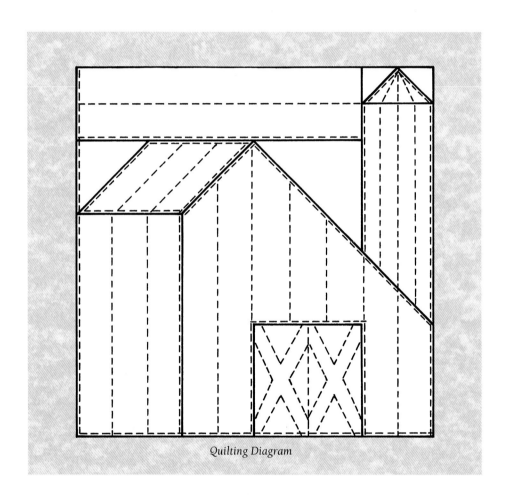

Quilting Diagram

Pintucked Nightie

MADE BY FAY KING

This pretty nightie shows another way to use traditional pinstitch and pintucking in an easy-to-make project.

Materials

- ♣ 2.2 m (2³/₈ yd) of Liberty print fabric
- ♣ 1 m (1¹/₈ yd) of matching Swiss Nelona
- ♣ DMC Stranded Cotton, White
- ♣ 1 m (1¹/₈ yd) of 2.5 cm (1 in) wide embroidered Swiss lace edging
- ♣ one flat mother-of-pearl button
- ♣ Piecemakers crewel needle, size 9
- ♣ twin needle for the sewing machine
- ♣ pintucking foot for the sewing machine
- ♣ water-soluble marker pen
- ♣ ruler
- ♣ two rolls of Mettler 2-ply Heirloom Cotton to match the Nelona

Method

See the Pattern and the Pintucking Grid on the Pull Out Pattern Sheet.

Cutting

1 From the Nelona, cut two 15 cm (5⁷/₈ in) wide strips across the full width of the fabric. Set these aside.

2 From the remaining Nelona, cut a piece 40 cm x 50 cm (15³/₄ in x 19¹/₂ in) for the front yoke. Cut out the back yoke from the Nelona.

3 From the Liberty fabric, cut two 1 m (1¹/₈ yd) pieces for the skirt.

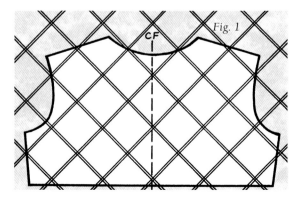
Fig. 1

4 Before cutting the Madeira appliqué 'collar' from the Liberty cotton, mark the scallops on the outer edge on the right side of the fabric and add a 6 mm (¹/₄ in) seam allowance. Cut out the collar on the fold.

Pintucking

1 Using the marker pen and the ruler, mark the pintucking grid on the front yoke, keeping all the lines straight.

2 Using the twin needle and the pintucking foot, stitch the pintucks in one direction first, then in the other direction. To stitch the echo pintucks, stitch again so the existing pintuck is sitting in the second groove to the left of centre on the pintucking foot. Stitch very slowly and keep the pintucks perfectly straight.

3 When all the pintucks are stitched, mark out the shape of the front yoke, placing the centre line through the points where the pintucks cross (Fig. 1).

Embroidery

Using two strands of cotton and following the stitch guide, embroider the granitos at the intersection of the pintucks. When the embroidery is complete, cut out the front yoke.

Assembling

1 Slash the centre back yoke to the pattern mark. Join the front and back yokes at the shoulders with French seams.

2 Matching the centre front and shoulder marks, pin the right side of the Madeira appliqué collar to the wrong side of the yoke. Sew around the neck edge with a 6 mm (¹/₄ in) seam. Clip into the curved seam allowance, then turn the collar to the right side of the yoke.

3 You can clip and baste the whole piece before you stitch the next step or you can work in small sections. At regular intervals, clip the outer scalloped edge of the collar to the marked line. Fold the clipped edge under and baste it in place.

4 Using a hand-pinstitch or a machine-hemstitch, complete the Madeira appliqué. For the pinstitch, use one strand of cotton and the crewel needle and follow the stitch guide.

5 Join the side seams with small French seams.

For the placket

From the Nelona, cut a strip of fabric 3 cm x 25 cm (1¼ in x 10 in). Press the strip over double, lengthwise. Pin the placket to the right side of the back opening, matching raw edges and turning a small hem at the top edges. Stitch, beginning with a 6 mm (¼ in) seam, tapering to a point at the base of the opening. Pivot at the point, then stitch along the other side to the opening, widening out to a 6 mm (¼ in) seam at the top. Turn the placket to the wrong side of the nightie and slipstitch the folded edge to the stitching line. Press.

For the armholes

1 Cut two 3 cm x 56 cm (1¼ in x 22 in) strips of Nelona on the bias. Press the strips over double.

2 Sew the binding to the right side of the armhole with the raw edges matching. Turn the folded edge to the wrong side of the nightie and slipstitch it in place.

For the skirt

1 Cut the two strips of Nelona set aside for the Madeira appliqué hem to the same width as the Liberty fabric. Join the Nelona into a loop with small French seams. Join the skirt pieces with small French seams.

2 Prepare the Madeira hem as for the collar, using the template provided. Join the right side of the Madeira hem to the wrong side of the skirt at the straight edge. Turn the Madeira hem to the right side of the skirt. Press the hemline carefully. Pinstitch by hand or hemstitch by machine to secure the Madeira hem.

Finishing

1 Cut the lace edging to the width of the skirt front plus 12 mm (½ in). Fold a tiny hem at both ends of the lace.

2 Pin the lace to the skirt front, then gather the skirt with three rows of gathering stitches. Pull up the gathering to fit the yoke, matching the seams and adjusting the gathers. Stitch the skirt to the yoke, using a 6 mm (¼ in) seam. Zigzag the edges to neaten them. Make a buttonhole loop at the back neck. Sew on the button to correspond.

Stitch Guide

Granitos

Run the thread through the fabric from **A** to **B** with very small stitches. The length from **A** to **B** should be approximately 3 mm (⅛ in).

Holding the end of the thread so it does not move, stitch from **A** to **B** three or four times, laying the stitches to the left or right of the centre. Place the last stitch over the centre.

Finish each granito on the back before proceeding to the next one. Do not carry any threads across the back of the work.

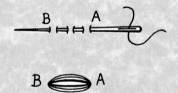

Pinstitch

Bring the needle up through the fabric at **A**. Secure it with a small backstitch.

Stitch through to the back of the fabric at **B**, then stitch from **B** to **C** on the back and **C** to **B** on the front. Then stitch from **B** to **D** on the back. Each stitch is approximately 3 mm (⅛ in) long. Stitch from **C** to **E** on the front, then **E** to **C** on the back and so on.

Make sure you use the same holes each time and pull each stitch firmly, but not too tightly or the fabric will pucker.

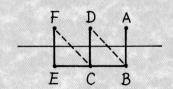

Baby's Sleeping Bag

STITCHED BY FAY KING

This sleeping bag is a wonderful way to keep your little one warm through the first winter.

Fits size: three to six months

Materials

- ❧ 1 m (40 in) of gown blanketing
- ❧ 1.7 m (1⅞ yd) of matching Swiss Nelona
- ❧ 4 m (4½ yd) of piping cord
- ❧ Appleton's Crewel Wool: White, Lemon, Pale Blue, Pale Green, Green, Light Brown, Yellow
- ❧ Pink Gossamer mohair
- ❧ Piecemakers tapestry needle
- ❧ transfer pencil
- ❧ eight buttons
- ❧ sewing thread to match the fabric
- ❧ tracing paper
- ❧ pencil

Method

See the Pattern and the Embroidery Design on the Pull Out Pattern Sheet.

Preparation

1 Trace the pattern pieces. Cut out the pattern pieces from the gown blanketing.

2 Transfer the main embroidery design onto one of the fronts so that the design sits 14 cm (5½ in) from the bottom edge. You will need to reverse the design for the other front.

Note: Take care when transferring the design that the iron is not too hot or you might scorch the fabric.

Embroidery

1 Stitch the swans and stems in stem stitch. Stitch the leaves in stem stitch, using Pale Green on one side and Green on the other.

2 Stitch the reeds and garlands in French knots.

3 Stitch the waterlilies in lazy daisy stitch placing two petals on each side and a fifth petal in the centre, overlapping the others (Fig. 1). For the centre of the waterlily, work three pistil stitches in Lemon.

4 Embroider the garlands on the collar piece, surrounded by leaves in detached chain stitches (Fig. 2). Stitch the forget-me-nots in Pale Blue French knots with Lemon French knot centres.

Sewing

1 Using the pattern, cut out the lining pieces from the Nelona. From the remaining Nelona, cut 3 cm (1¼ in) wide bias strips. Join them together then cover the piping cord with the joined bias.

2 Pin the piping to the right side of the collar around the scallops, 1 cm (⅜ in) from the edge. Clip into the seam allowance of the piping to allow it to curve gently but take care not to clip the stitching. Stitch the piping into place.

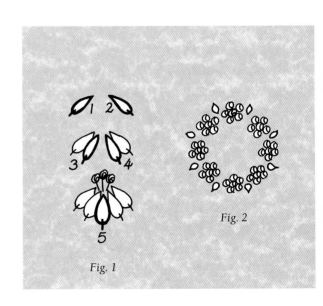

Fig. 1

Fig. 2

3 Place the collar and the collar lining together with the right sides facing. Sew them together around the scalloped edge, stitching in the stitching line of the piping. Clip both the collar and the lining, then turn the collar right side out. Press gently on the wrong side.

4 Join the fronts and back at the shoulders. Sew in the sleeves, then join the side seams. Make the lining in the same way.

5 Stitch the piping around the right side of the sleeve ends and around the front opening and the flap. Sew the collar to the neck edge, using a 1 cm (³⁄₈ in) seam.

6 Place the outer piece and the lining together with the right sides facing. Stitch them together around the sleeve ends, as close as possible to the piping stitching line, and around the front opening and flap edges. Do not stitch across the neck edge.

7 Turn the sleeping bag right side out through the neck opening. Fold over the seam allowance at the neck edge of the lining, clipping where necessary. Slipstitch the lining to the neck edge.

8 Make eight buttonholes and sew on the buttons to correspond.

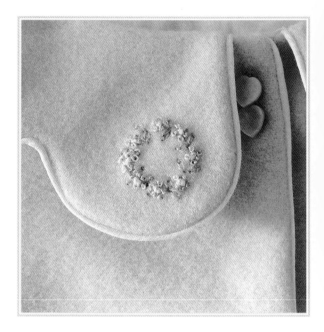

Chocolate Box

PAINTED BY LYN FOSTER

This dramatic black box, decorated with lush roses and touches of lace, provides wonderful storage with an elegant touch.

Materials

- ❧ 35 cm (14 in) round box
- ❧ white transfer paper
- ❧ stylus
- ❧ background paint, Black
- ❧ 5 cm (2 in) sponge brush
- ❧ round brushes, size 2 and size 4
- ❧ 6 mm (¼ in) dagger brush
- ❧ good liner brush
- ❧ Jo Sonja's Artists Acrylic Colors: Teal Green, Warm White, Pine Green, Burgundy, Storm Blue, Yellow Oxide, Brown Earth
- ❧ palette or old saucer

Method

See the Painting Design on the Pull Out Pattern Sheet.

Preparation

1 Using the sponge brush, base coat the box with two coats of Black, sanding the box lightly between coats. It is very important that you have a smooth surface on which to paint.

2 When the base coat is dry, trace the design from the pattern sheet and transfer the design to the box, using the transfer paper and stylus. Do not transfer the dots and the fine lines of the ribbon or lace.

Painting

1 Base coat the main ribbons and the lace insert with a mixture of Teal Green and Warm White, mixed to a light/medium colour. Make sure you keep the mixture smooth. When the base coat is dry, paint in the crosshatching, using the liner brush and Warm White. Do not paint any of the dots.

2 Base coat the bow with a lighter version of the ribbon base coat. Shade the ribbon with Teal Green. Dry brush in the highlights, using Warm White.

3 Base coat the leaves in a mixture of Teal Green and Pine Green. Using the same colour and the liner brush, paint in the stems.

4 Using the liner brush and a medium mix of Warm White and the leaf base colour, and starting at the tip of the leaf, pull strokes two-thirds of the way down the leaf. Add a little more Warm White to the mixture, then lighten the tips of the leaves with little fine lines.

For the roses

1 Base coat all the roses in a mix of Burgundy, Yellow Oxide and Warm White, varying the amount of Warm White to produce three different shades.

2 Using the dagger brush and a mixture of Burgundy and Yellow Oxide, float in the centre of the flowers.

3 Load the size 4 round brush with the base colour, side-loaded in Warm White. Pull in the back petals of the rose first, around the shaded centre, then paint the front and outer petals. When the petals are dry, dry brush in the highlight in Warm White.

4 Reinforce the centre of the roses using the dagger brush and Brown Earth.

5 Load the liner brush with Brown Earth and tip in Yellow Oxide, then pat in the stamen to the rose centre. Add highlights with a few dots of Warm White.

For the daisies

Paint the daisies in Warm White with a Yellow Oxide and Burgundy centre. Paint the directional dot in Warm White.

For the fillers

Paint the fillers in Storm Blue with a Warm White centre. Paint the directional dot in Storm Blue.

Finishing

Paint in the dots on the lace and ribbons, using the stylus.

Embroidered Brooch

EMBROIDERED BY JUDITH COOMBS

Stitch this tiny brooch as a gift for a special friend to wear or, as we have done, to frame as a nostalgia piece.

Materials

- ❧ gilt brooch frame
- ❧ small piece of silk fabric suitable for embroidery
- ❧ DMC Stranded Cotton: Pinks 223, 224, 225; Blue 800; Yellow 744; Greens 989, 936
- ❧ Piecemakers straw or milliners needle, size 9

Method

See the Embroidery Design below.

1 All the embroidery is worked using only one strand of cotton. Embroider the roses and rose buds first, then the forget-me-nots and, finally, the leaves. Work the stitches as indicated in the embroidery design.

2 When the embroidery is completed, make up the brooch following the instructions supplied with the brooch. We have framed this brooch on a background of velvet.

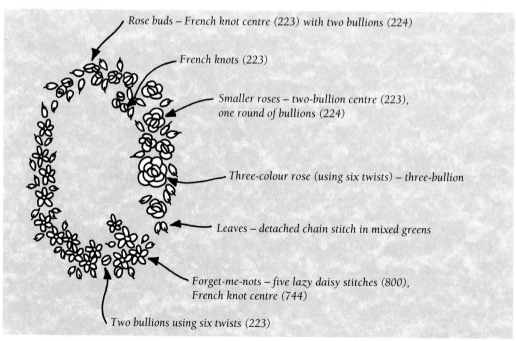

Rose buds – *French knot centre (223) with two bullions (224)*

French knots (223)

Smaller roses – two-bullion centre (223), one round of bullions (224)

Three-colour rose (using six twists) – three-bullion

Leaves – detached chain stitch in mixed greens

Forget-me-nots – five lazy daisy stitches (800), French knot centre (744)

Two bullions using six twists (223)

Heirloom Half-Slip

STITCHED BY PATRICIA HOLDEN

This delicate half-slip is the perfect project for an enthusiastic but inexperienced heirloom sewer.

Materials

Note: You will need to determine the length you wish your slip to be and adjust the fabric requirements accordingly.

- ❧ **1.5 m (1²/₃ yd) of 115 cm (45 in) wide fabric**
- ❧ **3 m (3¹/₃ yd) of insertion lace**
- ❧ **1.5 m (1²/₃ yd) of lace beading**
- ❧ **2.5 m (2³/₄ yd) of lace edging**
- ❧ **2 m (2¹/₄ yd) of narrow silk ribbon**
- ❧ **waist size plus 2.5 cm (1 in) of 7 mm (⁵/₁₆ in) wide elastic**
- ❧ **water-soluble marker pen**
- ❧ **lace-shaping board (optional), (cork board) or something similar**

Method

See the Pattern and the Lace-Shaping Pattern on the Pull Out Pattern Sheet.

1 Using the marker pen, trace the pattern onto the fabric for the front, placing the hemline approximately 5 cm (2.5 in) from the fabric edge.

2 Using the marker pen and the template provided, trace the lace-shaping pattern onto the same fabric, matching the centre front markings and the lower edge of the lace to the hemline of the half-slip.

3 Place the fabric onto the lace-shaping board. Beginning with the teardrops, pin a strip of the insertion lace to the outside of the teardrop and the connecting line. Cut the lace and recommence at the centre of the heart.

4 With two ends of the insertion lace together and using the marker pen, mark the mitre for the centre of the heart. Set the zigzag stitch on the sewing machine to 1.5 and stitch the mitred seam. Trim the lace close to the stitching and press.

5 Place the lace with the mitred seam in position on the heart. Beginning at the centre, pin the lace around the outside of the heart, across the lace at the bottom of the teardrops, and across to the side seams. With a very small straight stitch, stitch both sides of the lace to the fabric, stitching between the two outside threads of the lace heading. Follow the arrows on the template for the direction of the stitching. Do not stitch the centres of the teardrops or the lower edge of the insertion lace. Press.

6 Cut along the middle of the fabric behind the insertion lace. Clip into the raw edges, then press the raw edges towards the fabric so that they lie flat.

7 Set the machine for a very narrow zigzag with a stitch length of 0.5. Working on the right side, zigzag through both layers of fabric along the edges of the insertion lace. Allow the stitch to go off the edge of the fabric into the lace on one side and just catch the fabric on the other side. Trim the raw edges close to the zigzag stitching. Press the piece well. Trim away the doubled lace from behind.

8 Cut a 15 cm x 20 cm (6 in x 8 in) piece of fabric. Using a 1.6/70 twin needle, a very small straight stitch and a pintucking foot with the greatest number of grooves, sew pintucks 3 mm (³/₁₆ in) apart across the fabric. Press well.

9 Trace the teardrop shape twice onto the pintucked piece so the tucks run vertically. Cut two pintucked teardrops and insert them in the space under the unstitched edge of the insertion lace. Stitch the lace down, catching the pintucked piece as you go. Trim away the extra fabric beneath the tucks. Cut along the middle of the fabric behind the insertion lace. Clip into the raw edges, then press the raw edges towards the fabric so that they lie flat. Finish with zigzag stitching as before. Press well.

10 Attach a length of insertion lace to the back hem by straight stitching, then finish the raw edge with zigzag stitching as before.

Finishing

1 To join the side seams, using very small straight stitches, stitch a 6 mm (¹/₄ in) seam. Cut the top layer of fabric in the seam allowance back to 2 mm (¹/₁₆ in) and the bottom layer to 4 mm (¹/₆ in). Using a zigzag stitch with a width 4 mm (³/₁₆ in) and a length ³/₄, stitch along the seam so the

needle stitches into the fabric close to the seam line on one side and just off the edge of the fabric on the other side, causing the fabric to roll in towards the seam. Press the seam towards the back.

2 Using a zigzag stitch with a 2.5 mm (¹/₈ in) width and a length ³/₄, stitch the lace beading to the insertion lace at the bottom of the slip, gathering it ever so slightly at the curves on the front.

3 Gently pull the thread in the heading of the lace edging to gather it up, then using the same method as for the beading, attach the lace edging to the beading. Begin and end at one side seam, closing the lace with a flat seam by hand.

4 Thread the ribbon through the beading, tying bows where you wish.

5 Measure the desired length of the half-slip from the hem to the waist, allowing for a narrow casing. Trim, if necessary. Fold over 6 mm (¹/₄ in) at the top edge, then fold another 1 cm (³/₈ in). Press. Stitch the casing with a small straight stitch, leaving an opening at one side for inserting the elastic. Thread the elastic through the casing. Close the opening.

6 Embroider the centre of the heart, if you wish.

Silk Pillows

MADE BY GLORIA MCKINNON

These sumptuous little pillows can be used for brooches, hat pins, sewing pins or just as a wonderful decoration for your dressing table.

Materials

For each pillow

♣ 20 cm x 25 cm (8 in x 10 in) of Dupion silk
♣ polyester fibre fill
♣ stuffing tool

For the roses and lace pillow

♣ 2 m (2¼ yd) each of 12 mm (½ in) wide overdyed silk bias ribbon: Pink/Green, Dusty Pink, Autumn Pink
♣ 50 cm (20 in) each of 12 mm (½ in) wide overdyed silk bias ribbon, two Greens
♣ two guipure lace motifs
♣ Piecemakers crewel needle, size 9
♣ neutral sewing thread

For the rose spray pillow

♣ seven flocked rose leaves
♣ 2 m (2¼ yd) of 4 cm (1½ in) wide overdyed silk bias ribbon, Dusty Pink
♣ 1.5 m (1⅔ yd) of 4 mm (³⁄₁₆ in) wide silk ribbon, Pale Pink

For the buttons and lace pillow

♣ 50 cm (20 in) of 7.5 cm (3 in) wide cream guipure lace
♣ 1 m (1⅛ yd) of 4 cm (1½ in) wide vintage silk ribbon, Dusty Rose
♣ 50 cm (20 in) of 4 cm (1½ in) wide vintage silk ribbon, Green
♣ Perle No. 5 thread, 739
♣ craft glue
♣ 'antique' mother-of-pearl buttons in various sizes
♣ two brass hearts
♣ 1 m (1⅛ yd) of 4 mm (³⁄₁₆ in) wide silk ribbon, Cream
♣ neutral sewing thread
♣ long straw needle

Method

For all three pillows

1 Fold the Dupion silk over double so that it measures 12.5 cm x 20 cm (5 in x 8 in). Sew around three sides with a small machine stitch. To keep the corners square, stitch as shown in figure 1. Turn the piece right side out, making sure all the corners are pushed out completely.

2 Stuff the pillow very, very firmly. When you think it is properly stuffed, use the stuffing tool to push more stuffing down the sides and into the corners. This will ensure your pillow remains firm. Close the open side of the pillow with a ladder stitch.

Roses and lace pillow

1 To take the whiteness out of the lace motifs, dye them in a little strawberry tea.

2 Tie a neat knot approximately 2.5 cm (1 in) from the end of the ribbon (Fig. 2).

3 Holding the short end against the long end, tie off the top by winding thread around, just below the knot. This forms the centre of the rose (Fig. 3).

4 Fold back the top edge of the ribbon and begin rolling and folding until you have a pleasing rose-like shape. With each full turn, stitch through the base to hold the rose securely (Fig. 4). When the rose is completed, cut the ribbon and secure the last roll with stitching, leaving a long thread for attaching the rose. Make at least twelve roses.

For the rose buds

1 Fold the short end of a piece of Pink silk ribbon as shown in figure 5. Fold the other end over as shown in figure 6, then tie off the ribbon by winding around with thread.

2 Wrap the bud with Green ribbon and catch it securely at the base. Make at least six buds in this way.

For the leaves

Make five leaves in the same way as the rose buds, omitting the final step.

Finishing

Centre then stitch the lace motifs onto the top of the pillow. Pin the roses, leaves and rose buds around the motifs. When you are pleased with the arrangement, sew the leaves and buds on first, then attach the roses, working from the edge to the centre.

Rose spray pillow

1 Make two roses in the same way as the roses on the Roses and Lace pillow.

2 Arrange the leaves on the pillow, using pins to hold them in position. Place the roses amongst the leaves, then stitch the leaves to the pillow, using the sewing thread.

3 Cut the silk ribbon in half and fold it into loops and tails. Stitch the ribbon under the roses, then stitch the roses into place. You may need to catch the petals into place with a couple of small stitches.

Buttons and lace pillow

1 Cut the lace into two lengths which will fit around the pillow, following the shape of the motifs in the lace. Stitch the lace to the pillow, covering it completely and having the ends of the lace meet on the back of the pillow.

2 Make one rose, two buds and one leaf, following the directions given for the Roses and Lace Pillow. Stitch them to the top of the pillow, using the long needle.

3 Using the Perle thread, stitch through the buttons, tying off the thread at the back. Glue the buttons into position around the rose.

4 Thread the silk ribbon between the fabric of the pillow and the lace up to the side of the rose. Attach it to the rose with tiny stitches. Thread a heart, then tie a bow. Trim the ribbon ends. Attach the second heart to the other side of the rose.

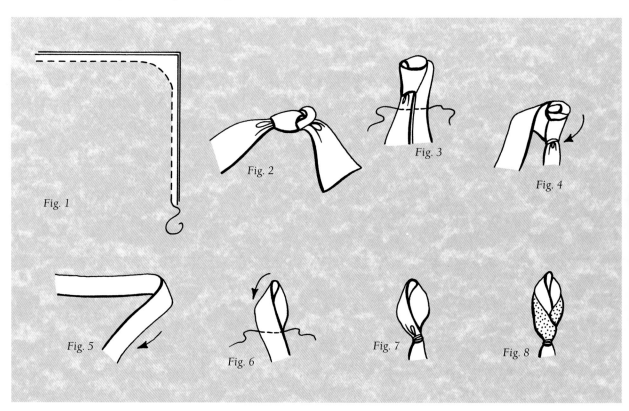

Fig. 1

Fig. 2

Fig. 3

Fig. 4

Fig. 5

Fig. 6

Fig. 7

Fig. 8